OUTPATIENT TREATMENT OF CHILD MOLESTERS

Stan Friedman, PhD

Chief Clinical Psychologist
Bureau of Clinical Services
Department of Corrections
Hudson, Wisconsin

Professional Resource Exchange, Inc.
Sarasota, Florida

Professional Resource Exchange, Inc.
635 South Orange Avenue, Suites 4-6
Post Office Box 15560
Sarasota, FL 34277-1560

Printed in the United States of America

Paperbound Edition ISBN: 0-943158-65-6
Library of Congress Catalog Card Number: 90-50824

The typist for this book was Denise Landi, the copy editor was Patricia Hammond, the proofreader was Karen Whatley, the managing editor was Debbie Fink, the graphics coordinator was Laurie Girsch, and the cover designer was Bill Tabler.

DEDICATION

To my wife, Jeri, who continues to inspire me.

PRACTITIONER'S RESOURCE SERIES

Outpatient Treatment of Child Molesters

Florence Kaslow, PhD
Director, Florida Couples and Family Institute
West Palm Beach, Florida

Peter A. Keller, PhD
Chair, Department of Psychology
Mansfield University
Mansfield, Pennsylvania

R. John Wakeman, PhD
Head, Department of Clinical Psychology
Ochsner Clinic and Ochsner Foundation Hospital
New Orleans, Louisiana

SERIES PREFACE

As a publisher of books, cassettes, and continuing education programs, the Professional Resource Exchange strives to provide mental health professionals with highly applied resources that can be used to enhance clinical skills and expand practical knowledge.

All of the titles in the *Practitioner's Resource Series* are designed to provide important new information on topics of vital concern to psychologists, clinical social workers, marriage and family therapists, psychiatrists, and other mental health professionals.

Although the focus and content of each book in this series will be quite different, there will be notable similarities:

1. Each title in the series will address a timely topic of critical clinical importance.
2. The target audience for each title will be practicing mental health professionals. Our authors were chosen for their ability to provide concrete "how-to-do-it" guidance to colleagues who are trying to increase their competence in dealing with complex clinical problems.
3. The information provided in these books will represent "state-of-the-art" information and techniques derived from both clinical experience and empirical research. Each of these guide books will include references and resources for those who wish to pursue more advanced study of the discussed topic.

4. The authors will provide numerous case studies, specific recommendations for practice, and the types of "nitty-gritty" details that clinicians need before they can incorporate new concepts and procedures into their practices.

We feel that one of the unique assets of the Professional Resource Exchange is that all of its editorial decisions are made by mental health professionals. The publisher, Larry Ritt, is a clinical psychologist and marriage and family therapist who maintains an active independent practice. The senior editor, Peter Keller, is a clinical psychologist who currently serves as chair of a psychology department and is actively involved in clinical training.

The editor of this series, Hal Smith, is a clinical psychologist in independent practice. He holds a diplomate in clinical psychology from the American Board of Professional Psychology, a diplomate in forensic psychology from the American Board of Forensic Psychology, and a diplomate in clinical neuropsychology from the American Board of Professional Neuropsychology. His specialties include clinical and forensic psychology, neuropsychology, stress management, management of chronic pain and psychophysiologic disorders, learning disabilities, interventions for spouse abusers, psychotherapy, psychodiagnostic evaluations, clinical hypnosis, and consultation.

We are also fortunate to have the services of an exceptionally well-qualified panel of consulting editors who assist in the selection and preparation of titles for this series: William D. Anton, Judith V. Becker, Philip C. Boswell, Florence Kaslow, and R. John Wakeman. Our consulting editors are all highly experienced clinicians. In addition, they have all made significant contributions to their professions as scholars, teachers, workshop leaders, researchers, and/or as authors and editors.

Lawrence G. Ritt, Publisher
Harold H. Smith, Jr., Series Editor

ABSTRACT

Most psychotherapists are generalists and therefore unlikely to possess any specific expertise for treating child molesters. Nevertheless, the clinical literature is almost always written with the specialist in mind. How is a therapist to respond on those occasions when he or she is faced with a child molester as a client? This guide addresses that question. It explains the role of the therapist in the larger criminal-justice system. It also offers guidance in the assessment process and suggests guidelines for deciding between outpatient and residential treatment. The author presents a series of sequential modules that are easily adapted to almost any style of therapy and encompass a complete primary treatment program. Finally, the appendix offers a listing of helpful resource material and support organizations.

TABLE OF CONTENTS

OUTPATIENT TREATMENT OF CHILD MOLESTERS

INTRODUCTION

Most psychotherapists are forced by both personal inclination and the diversity of clientele to be eclectic and generalist. It is impossible to be an expert in all of the specialty areas within the field of psychotherapy (Laws, 1988; E. L. Rowan & J. B. Rowan, 1985).

When problems suggest specialized treatment, the clinician might seek out assistance from a therapist possessing such skills (Knopp, Rosenberg, & Stevenson, 1986). However, such help may not exist. We may practice in a setting (e.g., prison, mental hospital) that does not readily permit or facilitate such consultation or referral. Similarly, we may practice in a geographical area with limited resources and/or a limited number of clients presenting with a specific problem, thus discouraging specialization of services (both in terms of staff specialization and program development). In such situations, we are, in a very real sense, forced to do the best we can under the circumstances (Moore, Zusman, & Root, 1985).

We may read the available literature and become aware of the state of the art (Greer & Stuart, 1983; Knopp, 1984; Money, 1987), yet how are we to translate that awareness into a viable treatment approach? I have observed that, under such circumstances, the nonspecialist therapist is likely to revert to the familiar and, in effect, avoid the specific problem. Many child molesters, for example, present with marked anxiety and/or depression. This is to be expected and seen as an appropriate reaction to their legal situation. Though they may require some supportive counseling, it is important not to place the focus of treatment on the depression, for example, and avoid dealing with the dynamics of the sexual offending.

This guide focuses on the assessment and treatment of clients who have had sexual contact with minors and is targeted to non-specialist psychotherapists, of whatever background, who sense a resonance with the preceding description. It attempts to do this in a realistic and sequential manner, paying careful heed to where the therapist's role fits contextually in the broader picture, which often involves the family, social service agencies, and the criminal justice system (Russell, 1984). In this guide I have avoided discussions of theory, preferring a "cookbook" approach.

There is a growing body of literature available (Barnard et al., 1989; Carnes, 1983; Cook & Howells, 1981; Finkelhor, 1984, 1986; Lanyon, 1986b; Mayer, 1988; Quinsey, 1986; Salter, 1988; Wolf, 1984) that can acquaint the reader with the accumulating panorama of theories, hypotheses, and data regarding child sexual abuse. This guide is not an exhaustive survey of treatment techniques. It omits those which, in the opinion of the author, are best left to institutional settings and/or specialists. It attempts to provide the reader with an understanding of "what to do" when practicing without either specialized knowledge, skills, resources, or ready access to someone who has such knowledge and skills.

The author has been a practicing, full-time licensed clinical psychologist for 22 years. A correctional psychologist for 18 years, he has specialized in the assessment and treatment of sex offenders in an outpatient setting for 10 years.

WHO IS A CHILD MOLESTER?

"The man has a secret. He's afraid to see his grandchildren because he fears he might molest them. 'It's weird, I know,' the white-haired man said, staring at his feet. 'But I've got these urges, and I can't control myself'" (*Milwaukee Journal*, 1/18/84).

"I am a 40-year-old white male that has had sexual contact with 120 to 130 boys with an average age of 13-1/2 . . . I think my end of the story should be told. I would like to talk about how I actually go about picking a boy up and how the boy is handled once contact has been made" (*Chicago Tribune*, 5/29/85).

"He's 51 years old and convicted in Burnett County of raping his teen-age daughter and molesting her younger sister.

"For the crimes, first-degree sexual assault, second-degree sexual assault, and reckless use of a weapon, he served nine months in the county jail, with five years' probation.

"'He needs help,' his former wife said. 'They don't take it seriously. It was treated like a domestic thing, just a domestic thing'" (*Eau Claire Leader-Telegram*, 10/18/85).

The term "child molester" is not a clinical label. It is a popular term used to describe someone who has had sexual contact with a child (Becker et al., 1986; Cook & Howells, 1981; Knight, Carter, & Prentky, 1989; Lanning, 1986; Quinsey, 1986). The clinical term "pedophile" is used to describe an individual who has a sexual attraction to children. However, the *DSM-III-R* (American Psychiatric Association, 1987) notes that "Isolated sexual acts with children do not necessarily warrant the diagnosis of Pedophilia. Such acts may be precipitated by marital discord, recent loss, or intense loneliness. In such instances the desire for sex with a child may be understood as a substitute for a preferred but unavailable adult" (p. 285).

Lanyon (1986b) offers a definition that disregards issues of gender preference and intrafamilial versus extrafamilial factors. He notes: "Child molesters tend to be defined as older persons whose conscious sexual desires and responses are directed, at least in part, toward dependent, developmentally immature children and adolescents who do not fully comprehend these actions and are unable to give informed consent" (p. 176).

From the therapist's vantage point, the value of any diagnostic label lies primarily in what guidelines it offers for treatment (Hall, in Barnard et al., 1989). The research literature tends to divide offenders against children into several overlapping categories: exclusive versus nonexclusive attraction to children; nonfamilial versus familial victims; violent versus nonviolent offense; pre-pubertal versus post-pubertal victims; homosexual versus heterosexual victims; and multiple victims versus single victim. It is widely accepted that change is more difficult for those offenders presenting a preponderance of the first of the above paired factors. The most resistant to change would be the client with an exclusive attraction to violent sexual interaction with extrafamilial, multiple, pre-pubertal, same-sex victims (Hobson & Bunk, 1987).

The first issue to consider is whether treating the offender in an outpatient setting presents too great a risk to the community

(G. Kaplan, 1988; W. R. Smith & Monastersky, 1986). The clinician should always be aware of the delicate line between concern for safety of the community and concern for measured positive change in the offender. Failure to conscientiously balance these concerns leads to increasing risk that a client may reoffend while in treatment (Quinsey, 1983). In addition to the obvious tragedy, this will lead to questions regarding the clinician's credibility.

Thus, in deciding whether to treat the offender in an outpatient setting, it would be wise for the clinician to use the previous factors as a screening mechanism (keeping in mind that they are not foolproof). No formula exists for reaching a decision after weighing these factors, and rarely does one factor by itself warrant reaching a definite conclusion. Under all but the most unusual circumstances, it would, however, be wise to avoid outpatient treatment for an offender whose sexual contact included elements of violence. Likewise, one would be wise to be cautious in accepting for outpatient treatment an offender who reoffended after having already completed a credible treatment program for sex offenders. Remember: The lower the likelihood of positive change, the greater the likelihood of recidivism.

Finally, keep in mind that it is neither appropriate nor possible for the clinician to use the assessment process for a determination of guilt or innocence. That determination is for the court (Friedman, 1989; Melton & Limber, 1989). If the client insists he is innocent, the evaluation should focus on personality description without expressing opinions as to his guilt or innocence.*

Of course, his protestation of innocence does not automatically preclude presentation and discussion of the treatment modules regarding the dynamics of child molestation. They can be used in the framework of hypothetical behavior. The therapist-client interaction will likely be restricted, but the offender may still benefit from exposure to the salient information. In reaching a decision as to whether to use this option, it is important that the therapist first consider the level of risk to the community, the implications of the "message" conveyed, and the other alternative dispositions available.

---

*Although children who are victims of child abuse may be either male or female, the overwhelming majority of offenders are male. Therefore, in this guide, I have used the masculine pronoun when referring to an offender and both feminine and masculine pronouns when referring to victims.

THE CLIENT WHO HAS NOT ACTED OUT

A client who has never sexually acted out may report to you that he is having fantasies or impulses to have sexual contact with a minor (Wegner, 1989). First, under most circumstances, there is no need to report this to the authorities. If, however, the client indicates a specific victim, and reasonable professional judgment suggests that the child is at risk, state law may require that you warn the potential victim. Second, the immediate goal should be to control acting out rather than focus on personality change (T. A. Smith & Conte, 1986).

As obvious as it may appear, many clients do not, on their own, recognize that the surest way to control their impulse is to avoid or remove situational opportunity: that is, to make a deliberate effort to avoid being in physical proximity to potential victims. This "buys time" to work on other issues.

The issue of situational opportunity should be reviewed in detail. Anticipate potentially troublesome situations instead of merely waiting for the unknown. Do not rely on spur-of-the-moment problem solving; use behavioral rehearsal. With the client, anticipate his day, focus on any situations which may provide him with the opportunity to act on his fantasy/impulse, and plan alternative, appropriate behaviors.

Suppose, for example, he has been having sexual fantasies of his daughter. It would be prudent for him to avoid situations that provide him unsupervised access to her. If he had intended to drive her somewhere, he might attempt to arrange for his spouse to do it instead. If this substitution proves to be inconvenient, then he should carefully plan and rehearse, mentally, appropriate ways of behaving with her. Consider this to be crisis intervention before the crisis!

Next, do not assume he is aware of the laws prohibiting sexual contact with a minor. Clients' knowledge runs the gamut from believing that such contact is allowed as long as the child's parents do not object and no force is used, to misunderstandings regarding appropriate age requirements. The therapist should become familiar with relevant statutes regarding age of consent (Kourany, Hill, & Hollender, 1986) and legal sanctions (e.g., the possibility of a felony charge and a prison term). It is important for the client to understand that acting out the behavior he has fantasized could lead to jail or prison. Discuss the embarrassment he would experience when his behavior was made public.

Emphasize that, despite what he might prefer to believe, there is no certain way to insure secrecy. There are many circuitous (as well as direct) paths by which information about child molestation reaches the authorities. Do not be afraid to create some anxiety regarding aversive consequences that may follow acting out; in most cases, anxiety is a valuable deterrent.

Be sensitive to the possibility, however, that for some clients, anxiety may serve to heighten arousal. This seeming paradox may reflect a significant deficiency in ability to develop victim empathy and predict a reduced likelihood of successful treatment.

Also, it has been my experience that the client appreciates accurate information. It helps him place his fantasy/impulse in a realistic context. Otherwise, it is too easy for him to focus on his fantasy/impulse as not really being "that serious," not really being a crime. Then, he is likely to minimize or avoid any consideration of the devastating effect it may have on his life. I recall a client who, while being evaluated as part of a pre-sentence investigation, described to me how he molested his stepdaughter while watching the local news on television. On the news was a feature story of a trial for child molestation! He noted that he experienced a brief feeling of anxiety but was quickly able to recover his equilibrium and reassure himself that what he was doing was "different." As will be discussed further in the section on "Denial, Rationalization, and Minimization" (pp. 21-23), it is important to give the client the knowledge and encouragement to view his fantasy in a realistic context, avoiding, as much as possible, access to unconflicted mental distortions.

Though it may be tempting at this point to attempt to discuss issues relating to the damage his behavior would cause the potential victim, it is best to avoid such a focus for the time being. Most offenders against minors are very self-centered; they are more likely to respond to concerns about how their behavior would affect themselves. Be specific! In a matter-of-fact manner, explain that there are many ways (some he could not predict) in which his behavior might be made public. If you have examples, use them! Point out that he would be criminally charged and prosecuted. Note the embarrassment to himself and his family. Discuss jail/prison and probation. Remind him that as long as he does not act out, you will both have time to work on his problem. Also, emphasize and reinforce in a positive way the strength and good sense he has demonstrated by recognizing and sharing with you the appropriate concerns he has regarding his fantasies.

YOUR RELATIONSHIP WITH THE CRIMINAL JUSTICE SYSTEM

Your relationship with the criminal justice system becomes, in essence, a relationship of roles (Barnard et al., 1989; Mayer, 1988; Salter, 1988). You may be dealing with child-protection workers from the county social service department, investigators from the police and/or sheriff's department, prosecuting attorneys from the district attorney's office, defense attorneys, the court, and probation agents. Your contact with these agencies will depend on your role in the case and who seeks your services.

The most common sequence of events begins with a report of abuse to the county social service agency (though it may, on occasion, be initially reported to the police). At this point, the social service agency's responsibility is to determine if the report is "founded" (i.e., likely to be true). If the report is "founded," then a referral may be made to the district attorney's office for criminal charging. Depending on the community, the alleged offender may already have been interviewed by the police.

Besides pleading "guilty" or "not guilty," several other options exist (these may differ among various jurisdictions) and may have an impact on the clinician's role. A *no contest* or *nolo contendere* plea indicates that the defendant chooses not to challenge the charge; he is neither admitting nor denying guilt. This plea has some potential utility for him should he also be charged in civil court (for emotional damage to the victim, for example). Of more immediate concern to the clinician is whether, despite the no contest plea, the offender has given a useful, reasonably detailed confession.

Another option in some jurisdictions is the Alford plea, whereby the defendant, in effect, proclaims his innocence but concedes that the evidence is such that he would, without doubt, be found guilty by a judge or jury. For the clinician's purposes, this client should be treated as one who has pled not guilty and maintained his innocence.

Though rarely used in such cases, the defendant may plead not guilty by reason of mental disease or defect (commonly referred to as the "insanity plea"). As noted previously, the clinician is advised to become familiar with his or her state statutes.

Finally, the district attorney has the option of deferring prosecution of the offender. Essentially, this involves a contract whereby it is agreed that if the defendant fulfills agreed-upon conditions, the charges will be dismissed. In child molestation cases, one of the imposed conditions is virtually certain to be "counseling." As a result, the clinician will be expected to keep the monitoring agency (most likely the district attorney's office) informed as to the status of treatment, including notification of the defendant's regularity in keeping appointments, participation in the treatment process, and level of risk for recidivism (Gable, 1986; Rencken, 1989).

It is important that you not perform your assessment under the assumption that the client is guilty if he professes innocence. Certainly he may be guilty, yet such a legal determination is not your responsibility or within your area of competence (Friedman, 1989; Melton & Limber, 1989). Further, such a mental framework is likely to bias your clinical judgment in the areas you are attempting to assess. You are likely to mentally label him, even if only to yourself, as "lying." This assumption of "defensiveness" may then skew your interpretation of test results, verbal statements, and behavior samples or reports (Lanyon, 1986a).

Make certain that you clearly understand your role at this point, explain it to the client, and observe appropriate standards of confidentiality. Be clear regarding the differing expectations of your role as an evaluator or a therapist. In your role as an evaluator, you will be assisting others in making a determination as to criminal disposition. They will be seeking help in answering such questions as these: Is he a high risk for recidivism? Is he suffering from a major mental disorder? Does he understand his situation? Is he competent to assist in his own defense? Is he a good candidate for treatment? You may be called on to testify in court. Be prepared to clearly explain your conclusions. Do not use any psychometric instrument to reach conclusions for which the instrument is not designed; a knowledgeable attorney may destroy your credibility during cross-examination (Brodsky, 1977). Finally, do not act as an advocate. Present your findings as objectively as possible, and do not overstep your limits of competence or knowledge.

If you see the offender in treatment, it is likely that at some point you will be asked for a recommendation regarding some type of dispositional decision. Some examples of such decisions are: Should he be allowed to be around minors unsupervised? Should he have his level of probation or parole supervision relaxed? Should he receive an early discharge from supervision? I strongly recommend that you avoid making such recommendations. It seems to me that, after working intensely with a client over a period of time, the clinician is likely to feel a certain rapport and empathy for the offender and may unwittingly become an advocate. Similarly, we would like to believe we have done a good job in counseling and may tend to overrate the offender's progress. Rather, it is more prudent (and probably less likely to expose the clinician to any legal liability) to provide an objective and complete progress report to others (even other clinicians), letting them make such critical decisions.

Before beginning an assessment, obtain all background material: police reports, victim's statement, defendant's statement, and criminal complaints. Study these materials, if possible, before seeing the client. At the very least, review them before completing your assessment. If possible, as part of the assessment process, interview the spouse (or significant other) of the offender. In this way, you may gain valuable insights regarding the offender's daily routine and his behavioral and attitudinal patterns.

If you are intending to see the client in ongoing treatment, relax any pressure you may feel to learn everything pertinent about the client at the first meeting. Encourage the development of trust and rapport. Be clear in explaining to the client what the limits for confidentiality may be, and be explicit in describing the child abuse reporting laws operative in your state. Confidentiality may well be limited statutorily. Further, court-ordered treatment (or treatment as a condition of probation) may require your sharing information with a representative of the criminal justice system. If you are not prepared to do this, your treatment may not satisfy the client's mandated condition, and he may be required to seek treatment elsewhere (American Psychological Association [APA], 1981; Jagim, Wittman, & Noll, 1978; McGuire, Toal, & Blau, 1985; Muehleman & Kimmons, 1981). This issue should be addressed at the outset.

THE SEX OFFENSE INTERVIEW

[After finishing this guide, the clinician will readily see how the questions in this interview provide specific information related to the individual dynamic factors discussed. This interview is not to be considered all-inclusive. As is suggested in the section on testing, the clinician should include consideration of other factors such as neurological and intellectual functioning and medical status as part of the evaluation.]

- Please describe the offense. (Note any divergence from victim's statement or police reports.)
- Why do you think it happened? (Deliberately use passive statement; see if he takes responsibility and to what degree.)
- Tell me about any discussions of a sexual nature you may have had with the victim. Did you view pictures or movies with explicit sexual content, and so on, with the victim?
- Tell me about any feelings you may have had of wanting to get "closer" to the victim but not have sexual contact.
- Did you feel the victim would do anything you wanted? What made you feel that way?
- Tell me about any angry feelings you may have felt toward the victim.
- Tell me how you dealt with these angry feelings.
- Did you ever use physical force on the victim?
- Tell me about any fears you may have had that the victim would report you. How did you deal with it?
- Tell me about any threats you may have made to the victim.
- How old did the victim seem to you?
- How old was the victim when you first had sexual contact?
- How old did you feel yourself to be?
- How old were you actually?
- Tell me about any thoughts or feelings you had about being discovered.
- How did you deal with these thoughts and feelings?
- Tell me about any alcohol or drug use in which you may have been involved at the time.
- Tell me about any unusual stress in your life at the time (i.e., marriage, employment, health, etc.).
- When did you first become aware that you might end up having sexual contact with the victim? Why did you become aware at that time?
- Tell me about any promises you may have made to yourself to stop.
- What do you think prevented you from stopping?
- Between the times when you had sexual contact with the victim, what kind of thoughts did you have about what had happened?
- Did you feel the victim wanted you to stop or continue?
- What led you to feel this way?
- How do you think the victim felt?

- What effect, if any, do you think this experience has had on the victim?
- Do you think what you did is wrong? Why?
- How does this fit into your religious beliefs?
- Were you ever abused yourself? If not, were you ever involved in sexual activities you would rather not have been involved in? Why?
- What kind of fantasies have you had about sex?
- How do you feel about these fantasies?
- What turns you on?
- Do you know of any other members of your family who have either been abusers or victims? Describe.
- Do you ever worry about whether you will do it again?
- Do you think you need psychological help? In what way?

TESTING

Psychological testing may or may not be useful depending on what you hope to accomplish. There are no psychometric instruments (or psychophysiological instruments such as the penile-plethysmograph, for that matter) with which to assess guilt or innocence (Abrams, 1989; Annon & Robinson, 1989; Pithers & Gibat, 1985). There are a number of survey instruments which may help to systematize the collection of data regarding the client's background, fantasies, and impulses (Nichols & Molinder, 1984; Thorne, 1986). It is important to keep in mind, though, that these are merely organized collections of the client's statements, not necessarily the "truth." If possible, try not to rely only on what the client tells you. Take advantage of collateral resources. You may decide not to confront the client with any contradictions between what he tells you and information you have gathered from other sources, but this understanding will still enable you to evaluate his defensive system more accurately.

The client may be marginally more honest in his answers if there is a clear understanding that the information he provides to you will not be used to buttress or dispute any legal claims he may make as to guilt or innocence. The data should serve only as an aid in making decisions as to clinical disposition and/or treatment. Determination of guilt is a legal matter better handled by the judicial system than by clinical assessment.

The client, at least at the initial stage, is apt to be suspicious of the intentions of virtually anyone perceived as part of "the system" and reluctant to reveal information which he sees as potentially damaging to his legal interests. Note, for example, the results of a preliminary study (T. A. Smith, 1985) conducted at Northwest Treatment Associates (a community based residential treatment center for sex offenders in Seattle, Washington), wherein T. A. Smith found that "fifty out of fifty clients lied about their deviant histories during evaluation" (p. 4). Further, it is not uncommon for such a predisposition to be encouraged by defense counsel. Accordingly, it is important for the clinician to maintain a healthy skepticism regarding the information provided by the client and avoid serving as little more than a conduit transmitting as fact what the client presents.

Do not hesitate to seek collateral information. Such information is valuable under any circumstances but most critical in performing an assessment, where maintenance of rapport is not as important a factor as during treatment. However, at the pre-adjudication stage, it is important that you not comment to the authorities in a way that might imply either guilt or innocence. The client is presumed innocent. Limit your public judgments to indications regarding, for example, intellectual level of development, possible neurological impairment (Hucker et al., 1986), personality characteristics (taking special care to evaluate validity of the results), and whether he might benefit from treatment. Keep in mind that the client has a vested interest in attempting to fashion the test results to his legal advantage.

Though there are several classification systems for child molesters, research has failed to find any specific test profile of the child molester. There does not appear to be any consistent response pattern on psychometric instruments reflective of a predisposition towards child molestation (Friedrich, in press; Hall et al., 1986; Hobson & Bunk, 1987; Levin & Stava, 1987; Quinsey, Arnold, & Pruesse, 1980; Wolf, 1985).

THE ROLE OF PUNISHMENT IN TREATMENT

Child molesting is a crime, and the community has an obligation to apply aversive consequences to individuals who violate its standards. Punishment serves to signal to the offender that his behavior is inappropriate, harmful, and will not be tolerated (Newlund, 1985). It is not uncommon for the offender to insist that the initial inconvenience and humiliation of the investigation, charging, and arrest are sufficient punishment and that any further consequences would be cruel and redundant. This agreement is especially common with upper socioeconomic offenders.

Unfortunately, however, in many cases, the result of this initial involvement with the criminal justice system serves primarily to reinforce in the offender an already existing belief that he is the victim. Many offenders have told me that it was not until after having served a period of time in jail (the consensus seems to be that 6 months is the optimum in terms of usefulness) were they prepared to see themselves as having perpetrated criminal behavior. In many cases, the offender's initial reaction to incarceration is an intensification of feelings of self-pity and victimization. This is followed (when accompanied by counseling) by a more accurate and less narcissistic assessment of his own behavior and responsibility.

There is also the hope that the aversive consequences of his behavior will dissuade him from repeating such behavior. Unfortunately, in a large percentage of cases, punishment alone does not serve to prevent recidivism. Similarly, treatment without punishment also seems relatively ineffective in preventing further sexual acting out (Newlund, 1985; T. A. Smith & Conte, 1986). Punishment combined with treatment, however, appears to provide the lowest rate of recidivism. The probable reasons for this will be discussed in the section "Power and Control" (pp. 28-30).

In accord with the earlier admonition against becoming an advocate for the client, it might be best for the clinician to limit involvement in sentencing recommendations to statements regarding issues such as: (a) mandatory outpatient treatment, (b) drug abuse/alcohol treatment, (c) mandatory abstinence from drugs/alcohol, and (d) no unsupervised interaction with the child.

It would be appropriate to help educate judges and attorneys as to how punishment interacts with treatment in a more general way. Your role is that of clinician, not surrogate prosecutor or defense attorney. By remembering this, you will be less likely to end up defending untenable and inappropriate clinical positions. Further, it will serve to enhance your credibility with defense attorneys, prosecutors, and the court.

TREATMENT

The sections following the general discussion of treatment may be considered as modules. Each describes a specific area involved in the dynamics of child molesting and suggests ways in which to present the area to the client. Each is suitable for either individual or group treatment. The goal is to present the material in a personal way, tailoring it to the individual circumstances of the particular offender. At the same time, it is helpful to use examples (hypothetical or otherwise) outside of the offender's experience. This will serve to indicate both that he is not the only one to have committed such offenses (a notion common to offenders, despite the publicity given to such offenses) and that the principles he is learning are applicable across a wide range of situations and personalities.

Though it may be tempting, for reasons of economy, to try to cover only those modules that appear to be relevant to a specific client, I strongly discourage this approach. There is no way to know for certain which of the factors may be significantly contributing to a particular client's difficulties. The best approach is to cover all of the factors, suggesting to the client that he sort them out in his own mind and lend special emphasis to those which he finds to be of special relevance to himself.

The listed sequence is one which I have found to be effective (though not critical). I strongly encourage beginning with a discussion of the offense (in group treatment, the "Go Round") followed by "Causes and Cures" and "Denial, Minimization, and Rationalization."

Many offenders will attempt to distract the therapist from dealing with the offense by emphasizing their pressing need to discuss other issues, such as their feelings of depression. Such issues may be important, but keep in mind what the purpose of treatment is in this case. If, indeed, you intend to focus on issues other than the dynamics of sexual offending, keep this clear in your own mind and to any others, including the client, with whom you may be communicating in this case. In any event, make your own decisions regarding the goals and content of treatment; do not let the offender set the therapeutic agenda. Power and control are salient enough issues (discussed in another section of this guide, pp. 28-30) without introducing such a dynamic struggle into the treatment process. Also, keep in mind that treatment at most may insure only that the offender has the knowledge and skills (demonstrated through completion of homework assignments) to avoid recidivism. It does not offer any assurance that he will actively and appropriately use the information and skills.

Over time and unmonitored, it is not unusual for the offender's thought processes to gradually shift, increasing his level of risk of recidivism (Turkington, 1987). Substance abuse, of course, invariably tends to distort one's thinking, thereby greatly increasing the likelihood that all the material learned will serve virtually no purpose. Even assuming sobriety, however, there still exists, in every case, a significant risk of gradual thought deterioration. Accordingly, it is of critical importance that some form of relapse prevention be included as part of the total "treatment package."

INDIVIDUAL, GROUP, OR FAMILY THERAPY

Most clinicians who treat child molesters indicate their belief in the efficacy of group therapy (Barnard et al., 1989; Knopp, 1984; Mayer, 1988; Rouleau, M. Kaplan, & Reich, 1984; Salter, 1988). First, the presence of other offenders clearly indicates to the client that he is not alone in his difficulty, that others share the same problem. There is some evidence to suggest, incidentally, that a lower rate of recidivism is achieved when the group is heterogeneous with regard to the specifics of the offense (Peters Institute, undated). Apparently, the diversity of types of acting out is less likely to lead to mutual reinforcement of rationalizations and the perception of one's behavior as "normal." Further, treatment may be facilitated markedly by the presence of a co-therapist. A male-female team of co-therapists is especially effective in dealing with stereotypical client attitudes regarding gender-role, power, and control.

Secondly, the group modality facilitates mutual confrontation (the role model being provided by the therapist), breaking-down of defenses, problem solving, and support (when appropriate). Thirdly, in a group that is not time-limited (which admits new members and discharges old members), there is the advantage of the transmittal by old members to new members of a positive group culture involving procedures, expectations, goals, and obstacles. Finally, economies of scale permit lower fees, thus making treatment more readily available and facilitating group diversity along lines of socioeconomic status (Yalom, 1975).

Despite the above, it is unlikely that the nonspecialist clinician will have enough such clients in treatment at any one time to sustain a group approach. Experience suggests that the optimal group size is six or seven, with a range of four to eight.

Fortunately, the treatment areas noted in this guide are, in most respects, readily applicable to an individual treatment approach. Such an approach does, however, place the clinician in the position of having to be continually aware of striking a delicate balance among a number of factors, including: rapport, empathy, objectivity, skepticism, confrontation, and realistic concern for possible recidivism. In short, it is harder work! (And it is probably less effective.)

In cases of intrafamilial child molestation (Paveza, 1988), family therapy is often used as part of the total treatment process (Trepper & Barrett, 1986). It would be counterproductive to meet with the family together at the beginning of therapy. The offender is likely to be defensive, the victim anxious and angry, and the spouse pressured into forming an alliance with either the offender or the victim. Family meetings seem most productive when initiated after each family member has completed his or her primary individual or group treatment (O'Connell, 1986).

WORKING WITH OFFENDERS AND VICTIMS

Clinicians who work with victims tend to develop feelings of antipathy toward offenders. This is understandable. It is difficult to repeatedly hear stories of victimization, especially of children, without wanting to engage in what is referred to as "offender bashing." After all, these are the individuals who have committed these unspeakable crimes, who have abused these children.

It certainly is possible intellectually to understand that rehabilitating offenders is a noble enterprise; such rehabilitation may spare countless future victims. We may understand all the caveats regarding treating the offender with dignity, deploring the behavior rather than the person. In practice, however, it becomes a sometimes impossible task to function appropriately with both the victim and the offender. Ironically, the clinician may even find himself or herself empathizing with the emotional turmoil of the offender and then minimizing the significance of the abuse to the victim. This is countertherapeutic. The clinician should not become an advocate for the offender (Barnard et al., 1989).

Though it is necessary for the clinician working with offenders to have an understanding of the effects of sexual abuse on victims (Conte, 1985; Finkelhor & Browne, 1985; Lindberg & Distad, 1985), in practice, it will prove difficult for the individual clinician to work with both offenders and victims. Certainly, the clinician working with the offender should share (within limits of confidentiality) appropriate information and coordinate with the clinician working with the victim.

DURATION OF THERAPY

The literature abounds with largely unsupported statements indicating that sex offenders virtually always need long-term treatment, possibly as long as 2 years (Knopp, 1984). When treatment is in a prison- or forensic-hospital-type setting, practical considerations such as employment, scheduling, fees, family interaction (possibly supporting dual households if the client has been court-ordered out of the home), and "no-shows" are not significant. In a variation of "The Peter Principle," the duration of the program may be determined, at least partially, by the length of incarceration. In an outpatient setting, however, the above-noted considerations must be addressed and accommodated.

Rather than approaching the question of treatment duration in an abstract manner, it may be more productive for the clinician to focus on an approximation (taking idiosyncratic client characteristics into account) of how long it will likely take to cover all the material in the treatment syllabus thoroughly (including review of assignments and outside reading). A good rule of thumb for the "average" client would be to figure two sessions for each of the syllabus topics. Consider this to be primary treatment; avoid having long intervals between sessions. One session a week would probably be optimum for most clients. As noted elsewhere in this guide (pp. 37-38), primary treatment should be followed by some form of relapse prevention (Laws, 1989). This may be construed as secondary treatment and in most cases should be of longer duration than primary treatment. It may, however, be scheduled less frequently if necessary and, if at all possible, in a group setting. Such groups are available in many parts of the country. (See listing of support organizations in Appendix, pp. 39-41.)

THE "GO ROUND"

In group therapy, begin by asking each member of the group to tell the group, in as much detail as he wishes, of his offense (Barnard et al., 1989; Mayer, 1988; Salter, 1988). In addition to initiating interaction among the participants, this procedure provides the therapist with some notion of how the offender views his own behavior as well as how judgmental he may be of others. You will likely discern something of a "pecking order" as each client ranks in severity his own offense relative to other offenses. This is a destructive process because it may serve to help offenders minimize the seriousness of their own behavior.

The therapist should attempt to dilute this pecking-order effect by noting the fact that the seriousness of the offense is affected by many factors, not merely whether it involved intercourse (which tends to be ranked as most serious). Point out that some of the other factors involve physical coerciveness, age of the victim, frequency of abuse, and willingness of the offender to admit he is completely at fault, thereby ameliorating any guilt the victim may have taken on herself or himself.

Assuming you already have in your possession (and have read) copies of the police reports (including the victim's statement), be prepared to confront discrepancies and omissions. Keep your tone mild and unemotional. Strong confrontation at this point may serve only to force the client to "harden" his position. Your confrontation serves mainly to indicate to the individual (and the group) that you are aware of contradictions, have access to collateral information, and are not naïve.

Denial, minimization, and rationalization are common to child molesters, and the therapist should not be surprised to find significant discrepancies between a victim's and an offender's statements. Such discrepancies may be resolved as the group process continues, but their resolution is not necessarily critical to treatment. Remember, the treatment process is not a criminal investigation but an attempt to positively modify thought and behavior patterns.

In individual treatment, have the client describe his offense. Initially, many clients tend to avoid giving a description of their offense. Instead, they are likely to "talk legal-talk," making statements such as "I was charged with first-degree sexual assault." Reply that you were aware of that and have read the police reports but would like to hear, in the client's own words, just exactly what it was that he did. Focus on the level of behavioral description. The offender is almost certainly incapable at this point of adequately understanding the dynamics of his offense.

It is not at all uncommon for child molesters to become quite embarrassed when asked to describe their offense. They are likely to talk in very general terms, making statements such as "I had sexual contact with her," "We did it," or "I touched her where I shouldn't have." Both legal-talk and vague terminology are countertherapeutic. They assist and encourage the offender to avoid facing the personal and specific qualities of his behavior and its implications.

Likewise, it is important that you discourage description in the passive mode: "It happened." Insist that the client describe his behavior in a manner that makes it clear that "he did" something, that the behavior did not just happen by itself.

Discourage the offender from describing behavior as cooperative and conjoint: "We had sex." The language used should make clear that the offender abused the victim. At times, offenders will use statements such as: "We made love." This minimizes the manipulative, abusive nature of the behavior; such a description should be challenged. Explain why the language (and the concept it represents) is inappropriate and countertherapeutic.

It is important that you have the client present a reasonably accurate behavioral description of his offense (Salter, 1988). This may not be possible immediately, but it should be pursued during the early stages of treatment. Minor contradictions between his description and that noted in police reports or the victim's statement are generally of little consequence. Other issues may be of major import, however. For example, if his description omits or severely minimizes the degree of coercion or violence involved in the offense, the discrepancy is irreconcilable, and he insists on the accuracy of his version, you must be prepared at least to consider the possibility that there is too great a degree of risk in working with him in an outpatient setting.

In a similar vein, consider other situations. Suppose the victim indicates an extensive history of abuse by the offender, while the offender insists that "It only happened once." Suppose the victim notes that anal intercourse occurred, while the offender insists that "I only touched her on the outside of the vagina." You must consider whether the degree of defensiveness suggests that the client is not yet willing to deal with his inappropriate behavior (G. Kaplan, 1988).

CAUSES AND CURES

Probably the most frequent answer given by child molesters in response to the question regarding what they hope to learn in treatment is "The reason why I did it." They assume that there is a single factor and that that factor is "the cause." It is important that you not discourage their inquisitiveness, their genuine desire to better understand the etiology of their behavior. Keep in mind that they usually do want to change, but they do not know how.

Thus, child molesters tend to hope for some magical, simple (but elusive) factor that you can point out. Once they learn what this mysterious ingredient is, the reasoning proceeds, they need only eliminate it from their "diet," and they will be "cured," never having to worry about further acting out.

Point out that the "myth of the cause" is a common misconception. There are a number of factors that contribute in various ways to child molesting, and you will be making your client knowledgeable about each one (Finkelhor & Araji, 1986). Undoubtedly, not all the factors will be relevant to each client's situation and personality dynamics, but there is no certain way to determine beforehand which of the factors will be significant. Thus, prudence dictates that each client be made aware of all factors. The client may then give appropriate emphasis to those factors that seem especially relevant in his individual case.

Similarly, discuss the common "myth of the cure." Clients generally believe that once they have completed the present treatment program there is no possibility of their ever again molesting a child (Laws, 1989). They need to understand that there is always the risk of "slippage." They will be made to understand that thought patterns and behavior patterns are always subject to change. During treatment they will acquire the tools to help them become aware, at the early stages, of any destructive tendencies in their thinking and/or behavior. They will learn the appropriate remedial steps to take.

A useful concept to introduce at this point (and throughout treatment) is the "thermometer of risk." The range of probability readings on this thermometer is 0-100. A reading of 0 is impossible since it indicates that an individual is at 0% probability of acting out. This is an untenable position. It is important for the client always to consider himself to be at some level of risk, no matter how minimal. If he were to consider himself to be at 0% risk, he would likely consider himself "cured" and avoid relapse prevention. His goal is to keep himself at as low a level of risk on the thermometer as is reasonably possible. He will learn to assign weightings, in an approximate manner, to each of the contributory factors.

The higher the reading, the more difficult and stressful it will be for the client to take remedial steps. Each client will learn to sense his "comfort range." As he monitors his feelings, thoughts, and fantasies on an ongoing basis, he will become aware of significant shifts in his risk level. If possible, he may be able to resolve the factor leading to the increased thermometer reading. If this is not possible, then he should strive to reduce the impact of another factor, thus reducing the overall thermometer reading despite the specific impasse.

Suppose, for example, the client has just had an argument with his wife and is aware that his level of perceived stress has increased substantially. Further, he knows that this has in the past tended to lead him to seek out sexual contact with minors. For whatever reason he is, at present, unable to resolve the conflictful issues with his wife. He might reduce the thermometer reading by, for example, deliberately avoiding situational opportunity to interact with minors or by focusing his thoughts on victim empathy issues.

In essence, then, the offender needs to understand that there is no one "cause," and there is no final "cure." There are a number of contributing causative factors, and it is an ongoing process to monitor these factors and keep their impact within the safe "comfort range," thereby minimizing risk of recidivism.

DENIAL, MINIMIZATION, AND RATIONALIZATION

Many offenders do not readily, openly, and completely admit to their inappropriate behavior (Barnard et al., 1989; Mayer, 1988; Salter, 1988). It is usually helpful to them to more clearly understand and appreciate the reasons why they and others in their situation tend to "cover up" and distort. I have found it to be effective to present this factor as encompassing three separate (though, at times, overlapping) issues: denial, minimization, and rationalization. Each subfactor is presented separately, below. If the therapist has had insufficient actual experience with such clients to have accumulated a repertoire of illustrative examples, it would be suitable to present hypothetical situations. The important thing is that the client clearly understands the concepts and sees their relevance to his situation and experience.

Denial. There are two types of denial. The first is that usually implied in common usage: the implication that the individual is consciously lying. In the context of child molesting, the suggestion is that the client is consciously aware of his inappropriate behavior yet chooses to deny it to others. His motivation for such behavior is readily understandable. It is likely to involve such concerns as embarrassment, fear of family disruption, and fear of legal consequences.

The other form of denial is when the client represses memory of the behavior. He may vehemently deny any memory of the offense and insist further that it is not at all consistent with his self-image. It would likely be counterproductive to argue with him in an attempt to "prove" to him that he is guilty. Your efforts to do so would be more apt to increase his resistance and eliminate any possibility of developing a therapeutic rapport. The clinician may also feel ambivalent as to which type of denial process is operative.

If your "working hypothesis" is that repression is causing the denial, it would be appropriate to let the client know that it is not uncommon for people to "block out" memories that are difficult to accept. Explain that he may begin to remember more of what happened as treatment progresses. Provide a brief explanation of the phenomenon of repression. The important thing is to avoid rigidifying his defenses, to make it permissible for him to begin to remember his behavior. He needs to understand that if, indeed, he really does not remember much or all of what happened, that is not "proof" that he did nothing.

As treatment progresses, he will begin to understand more of the dynamics involved in child molestation and the control he is capable of exercising over his own fantasies, impulses, and behavior (Bays & Freeman-Longo, 1989; Carnes, 1983, 1989; Freeman-Longo & Bays, 1988; CompCare, 1987). This knowledge will tend to mitigate his deeply felt fear that he is unalterably "sick" and "perverted" (O'Brien, 1986; T. A. Smith & Conte, 1986). His increasing sense of self-control and loss of helplessness will make it safe for him to begin to remember. If, however, the client continues to claim innocence, it would be advisable to reconsider the appropriateness of continuing treatment. It may well be that he is consciously lying or that he is indeed innocent (Wakefield & Underwager, 1988).

Minimization. Not infrequently, one will find discrepancies between the victim's allegations and the offender's admission. He may admit some of the allegations but minimize the extent and/or frequency of molestation. In the early stages of treatment, it is likely to be futile to attempt to penetrate this defense in a confrontational manner. The offender is attempting to bolster his self-image by engaging in comparisons of his own behavior with both his internal standards of appropriate behavior and his evaluation of child molestation by others. He is creating a covert hierarchy (though in a group setting he may express it overtly) of child molestation and attempting to structure it so that what he did "isn't really that bad." As treatment progresses, and he has less need for this hierarchy, he will be more apt to fully own his behavior without any need for minimization.

As with denial, however, it is important that he have an understanding of this phenomenon. Present the explanation in a nonthreatening manner and explain that it is not at all uncommon. He needs to see himself as not being unique, to realize that he shares this characteristic defensiveness with many other people.

Rationalization. Even when the offender admits to the physical acts that are alleged by the victim, he still may become defensive in "explaining" his intent. He may insist that he received no sexual gratification, was merely giving health and/or sexual instruction, was checking the victim's physical condition, complying with the victim's desire (expressed or otherwise), "accidentally" touched the victim, and so on. The list of rationalizations seems virtually endless.

Here, again, confrontation is unlikely to dismantle the offender's defenses. Explain to him that such a phenomenon is common. Give him anecdotal examples. Gently emphasize that persisting with such rationalizations is likely to increase the probability of recidivism. Indicate that you understand that it is often difficult to admit one's true motives, especially when one has already rationalized one's behavior when explaining it to significant others. Note, however, that such an admission to oneself (to begin with) helps greatly in reducing even unexpressed feelings of guilt and self-derogation.

As treatment progresses, periodically inquire as to whether he is beginning to reach a clearer understanding of the motives which largely precipitated his unacceptable behavior. This approach will present him with the opportunity to more comfortably accept and verbalize his true motivation and reject his own rationalizations.

DISINHIBITION THROUGH SUBSTANCE ABUSE

Determine what part, if any, alcohol or drug abuse played in the offense (Jacobs, undated). If the role seems to have been significant (Hucker, Webster, & Ben-Aron, 1981), then this chemical dependency issue needs to be dealt with before involving the client in focused sex offender treatment (Barnard et al., 1989).

Treatment involves teaching the offender to modify both the context and structure of his cognitions. Quite simply, abuse of psychoactive substances will minimize, if not eliminate, the situational recall of such knowledge and will tend to disinhibit behavioral controls (Greer & Stuart, 1983). Though in some situations it may be necessary either to delay or to preclude chemical dependency treatment while the client begins sex offender treatment, this should not be considered the preferred sequence and will substantially increase the risk of recidivism (Russell, 1984).

THE SETUP

Offenders generally will insist that their abusive behavior was impulsive, unplanned, that they had no warning of what they might do. They may describe a feeling of helplessness, loss of control. They may in some cases ascribe responsibility to the victims, claiming that they actively seduced them. They may resort to attributing responsibility to supernatural forces such as "the devil." Except in those cases in which the offender is deliberately lying, he is likely to believe what he tells you, to feel out of control, and fear that his behavior is, finally, unmanageable (O'Brien, 1986).

Yet in most cases, it will be transparently clear, upon reconstruction of the events leading up to the abuse, that preparations of a sort were indeed made (Rencken, 1989). The victim may have been isolated, the offender may have entertained sexual fantasies of the victim, or an "innocent" discussion of sexual matters may have preceded the abuse. The point is that it is almost always possible retrospectively to learn how the offender begins to "set up" the conditions for his abusive behavior. Even if deliberate intent is not evident, behavior that clearly facilitates or enables the abuse will be discovered (Bays & Freeman-Longo, 1989; Freeman-Longo & Bays, 1988). The goal is not to ascribe blame but to learn how to recognize the warning signs.

Imagine a videotape recording of the offender's life preceding the abusive behavior. The period encompassed by the recording may be as brief as minutes or as long as weeks or months. At the beginning stages of treatment, if the offender were to view the tape, our presumption is that he would have great difficulty in recognizing relevant factors, situations, and behaviors triggering the abuse. He would likely continue to insist that his abusive behavior "just happened" without any clear warning. As treatment progresses, however, he will discern warning signs and self-enabling behaviors. Thus, he will be in a greatly enhanced position to shape and determine his own behavior. He will virtually eliminate the feelings of helplessness and greatly increase the feelings of self-determination and self-control.

A critical part of both assessment and treatment is to develop a detailed "tape." Gather details of the offender's life prior to the abusive behavior: stresses at work and at home, sexual frustrations and fantasies (including use of pornography), recreation (books, movies), "cruising" (i.e., looking for victims), and/or interpersonal relationships. Periodically, as treatment progresses, review the tape with the client, adding to it as he becomes aware of what appears to be relevant material. The sequence of relevant contributing or enabling factors comprises the setup. As he gradually recognizes his own setup, he will realize that his behavior only appears to be impulsive. In addition to his beginning to assume greater responsibility for his behavior, he will feel an increasing sense of self-mastery. The ultimate goal is for him to recognize as early in the sequence as possible those factors and situations that contribute to the increasing probability of "impulsive" abusive behavior. By recognizing them early, he is presented with the opportunity to resolve, modify, or avoid them (Pithers et al., in Greer & Stuart, 1983).

FANTASIES

Offenders often indicate that they are bothered by intrusive sexual fantasies of inappropriate behavior. Their attempts to distract themselves from or to ignore these fantasies have almost certainly proven useless at best and counterproductive at worst (Wegner, 1989). Over time, the intrusive fantasies may come to be feared, their approach precipitating a panic reaction in some cases. In other cases, the offender comes to accept the thoughts as inevitable. He may in fact positively reinforce his deviant fantasies through masturbation. In both situations, however, there is a feeling of helplessness, a sense of resignation. The offender concludes that it is useless to attempt to resist the fantasy. Further, he may conclude that the next logical step in the "inevitable" progression, the only way to reduce the stress he is feeling, is to act out the fantasy.

Rather than attempt to resist, suppress, or act out the fantasy, the offender needs to learn to "complete" the fantasy - to dilute and modify its impact by altering its normal course. Whenever the fantasy intrudes into awareness, he is to modify its content in a prescribed, rehearsed manner (Laws, 1985). He should insert into the fantasy a deliberate awareness of the various factors he will become aware of in treatment: manipulation of the victim; effects (long- and short-term) on the victim (these two factors will be effective only for those offenders who have a reasonable degree of empathetic concern for victims); awareness of the guilt he will likely experience; anxiety of being detected and reported to the authorities; embarrassment when his behavior becomes public knowledge; prosecution; and imprisonment. Detailed visualization of these factors and consequences is almost certain to remove the sexual excitement usually engendered in him by the destructive fantasies with which he has become familiar.

He may actively resist these exercises, finding it distressing to actively insert anxiety-producing material into stress-reducing scenarios. Emphasize the importance of these exercises (Shelton & Levy, 1981). Be firm and graphic in pointing out the dangers to the offender should he choose to retain his uncompleted fantasies.

Another technique used in an attempt to eliminate deviant fantasies is *masturbatory satiation* (Barnard et al., 1989). The goal of this technique is to minimize the sexually arousing qualities of the fantasies by associating them with aversive sensations. After masturbating to orgasm to a nondeviant sexual fantasy, the client attempts to masturbate to orgasm (during the refractory phase) for a prescribed period of time.

SEXUALIZATION OF INTIMACY

Humans are social creatures; we seem to have an instinctual drive to get close to others of our species. Yet, this drive is susceptible to distortions and sublimations. For many men, intimacy is closely associated with vulnerability (Segal & Marshall, 1985; Whitman & Quinsey, 1981). Vulnerability, in turn, is perceived as being dangerous, an experience to be avoided at all costs. For these men, however, sex is equated with power, control, and masculinity; thus, it is acceptable.

Many child molesters have an approach-avoidance conflict in dealing with intimacy. They resolve this conflict by substituting sexual contact for the closeness, touch, and affection that they deeply crave but fear. This understanding will help explain the apparent paradox when the molester insists that he truly loves children and would never do anything to harm them. In some of these cases, he truly believes it. He sees his contacts with them as nurturing and affectionate. I have seen offenders truly devastated by their first realization that they have abused a child.

In many jurisdictions, child molestation is charged under the category of sexual assault. The nonviolent offender who does not yet understand the emotional harm he may have caused his victim (possibly not even yet understanding that there was a "victim") will often prove quite resistive to an admission of sexual contact or a meaningful therapeutic dialogue because of his difficulty in satisfactorily resolving for himself the notion that he is being considered an "assaulter." In such cases, I explain that I believe the client did not assault (i.e., attempt to physically harm) the child. If the client seems to accept the fact that I understand his concern, an explanation is presented regarding the notion of psychological abuse, being careful not to minimize, exaggerate, dramatize, or go beyond what the offender can emotionally handle.

During this section, explore with the client his history, focusing on his experience with and attitudes about intimacy. Attempt to relate these experiences and attitudes to his perceived motivation and goals in his relationship to his victim. Certainly part of the therapeutic task is to assist him in learning to more appropriately satisfy his innate need for intimacy (Barnard et al., 1989; Salter, 1988).

SEXUAL CONDITIONING OF THE VICTIM

In those cases where sexual conditioning of the victim occurs, it may be thought of as akin to a "breaking-in" period (sometimes referred to in the literature as the "grooming process"). Consciously or otherwise, the offender senses that a sudden sexual approach to the victim, without preparing the victim emotionally and cognitively, would be met with resistance, whether physical or emotional. This knowledge triggers a degree of anticipatory anxiety that is allayed by behavior intended to prepare the victim for abuse. This behavior gradually accustoms the victim to increasingly intrusive, inappropriate sexual activities.

These activities may encompass a wide range of behaviors and situations (Emmerman, 1985). The offender may discuss inappropriate sexual matters (likely in an intrusive, uninvited fashion). He may introduce the victim to sexual media such as videos or magazines. He may dress in an inappropriately revealing way. He may insist (or arrange) that there be a lack of privacy by, for example, leaving doors ajar when partially or completely undressed. The schemes are myriad, but the goal is constant: to gradually accustom the victim to increasingly intrusive and inappropriate sexual behaviors.

One offender who was a shopkeeper encouraged neighborhood youngsters to "hang out" at his place of business, where he very deliberately (as he later admitted to me) kept issues of *Playboy* and *Penthouse* lying around on the tables. His intent was to stimulate sexual interest and curiosity among the children so as to facilitate his sexual overtures to them.

Similarly, it is common to learn from victims' statements that the offender encouraged them to participate in viewing pornographic videos. In addition to helping relax the guard of the potential victims to precondition them for more direct sexual experience, the "shared" participation in the activity (e.g., watching sexually oriented movies together) also serves to blur the differences in age and role expectations between the offender and victim (refer to the section on age merging, pp. 30-31). This facilitates cooperation by convincing the victim that the behavior is appropriate. It also serves to increase the likelihood that the victim will, unfortunately, perceive herself or himself as a consenting participant and will be less likely to report the abuse.

The therapeutic dialogue about this treatment module should emphasize its role in the "setup." The offender should become further disabused of any lingering notion he may have regarding the "impulsivity" of his deviant behavior. Explore with him his understanding of age/role-appropriate behaviors in interacting with minors. Include social skills training, as needed.

POWER AND CONTROL

Though not an uncommon phenomenon in most areas of life, the quest for power and control seems to hold special prominence among the factors contributing to child molestation (Russell, 1984). The offender may feel put-upon and misunderstood by adults. He may feel helpless in dealing with life (Rencken, 1989). He may feel sexually inadequate. Any one of these and similar situations may create stress associated with feelings of helplessness. Interacting with children offers a seemingly ideal way to reduce stress and gain self-reassurance and feelings of power, control, and potency.

There are a number of reasons why this is so (Russell, 1984). First, children are usually taught to submit to adult authority.

Thus, they are much less likely than adults to protest intrusive behavior. Second, in most cases they have little, if any, understanding of what are considered to be inappropriate behaviors; thus, they are very likely to doubt the validity of their own uncomfortable feelings. Further, the contact may feel pleasurable and thus engender a conflictual, confused perception of what is happening. Third, they may be easily led to (or self-generate) the conclusion that they precipitated or were equally complicitous in the contact. Fourth, were they to report what happened, there is a significant likelihood that they would be disbelieved. Also, they generally lack the conceptual understanding as well as the vocabulary to describe what happened. Fifth, having little or no previous sexual experience, they are unlikely to judge the sexual performance of the offender, thereby allaying his anxiety regarding inadequate sexual performance. Finally, children are more easily intimidated than adults about reporting such behavior. They are apt to credit with validity even the most unlikely or unbelievable threats.

There is a reciprocity operational or expected in most adult relationships, a give-and-take. Whenever this balancing factor is absent or inadequately represented, a degree of tension is almost certain to intrude. The participants may renegotiate or withdraw from their "contract." If these options are eliminated, however, the relationship will continue under conditions of a continuing struggle for power. This may range in style from brute force to the most subtle forms of manipulation. Some adults live with the belief system that all human relationships are "contests" involving "winners" and "losers." For these individuals, reciprocity is not a viable option. Adults feeling inadequate, harboring the belief that they will inevitably lose in adult struggles for control, are likely to withdraw from the arena. For them, the childhood arena is safer; it virtually insures their "winning." The style by which they "win" may vary, as indicated previously, from brute force to subtle manipulation. Those offenders using the latter modes of abuse are likely to initially resist acceptance of the notion that they have abused a child.

As to the frequently asked question of why for these individuals the quest for power and control leads to sex (rather than other areas of human contact), there is as yet no simple answer (Money, 1986). Certainly, though, there are few more satisfactory stress reducers than sex. Stress reduction is finally what we are talking about.

An offender serving a jail term with work-release privileges (as part of his sentence for molesting his daughter) arrived late for group therapy. Frustrated and angry, he explained that he had been ready to leave at the appropriate time but was stymied by the tardiness of the jail personnel in releasing him. Further, he exclaimed bitterly, the officer on duty had been "just reading a paperback . . . he could have gotten me out on time but was just pushing his authority!" This material was processed with him by drawing an analogy between the powerlessness he felt in the present situation and the powerlessness his daughter must have felt during the abuse.

In reflecting on the role of power and control in child molestation, we may come to understand why incarceration is almost always needed as an integral part of the treatment process (Newlund, 1985). Though therapeutic discussions may give the offender some intellectual understanding of the way in which he has usurped from the victim control over her or his own body, the affective component of his understanding is likely to be insufficient. By placing him in a position wherein others have direct power and control over him, the community facilitates his experiential development of empathetic understanding.

AGE MERGING

It is not uncommon for the offender to describe his victim in terms which seem to defy credibility. He may explain that it would be misleading to think of his victim as a stereotypical 9-year-old, for example. She, as he sees it, is mature, intelligent, sophisticated, and sensual. She certainly was capable of giving consent and was, in fact, a sexual partner rather than a victim. He very likely is completely sincere in his protestations. Further, he may even encourage you to "see for yourself." He is thoroughly convinced that any open-minded observer would see things as he does. Those who are prosecuting him are undoubtedly malicious in intent or else merely sticklers for the technical letter of the law.

If one pursues this line of inquiry, an interesting phenomenon often begins to emerge. Ask the client to estimate the age he perceives his victim to be in terms of emotional and/or physical development (for the moment, disregard chronological age). Then, attempt to determine an estimate of his own "experienced" age. At what level of emotional development does he seem most comfortable, if not fixated? To what age does he wish he could return (while retaining the knowledge/experience advantage he has amassed, of course)? Likely, you will discover a minimum differential between the perceived age of the victim and the experienced age of the offender. This greatly reduced differential facilitates the operation of the mechanisms of rationalization and minimization (noted in an earlier section, pp. 21-23). This factor is well-described as age merging.

A 34-year-old male was referred to me for evaluation as part of a pre-sentence investigation for the court. He had been having sexual relations with a 13-year-old female and had then violated his bond (which included a restriction against any further contact with her) by meeting with her at a motel.

This offender was married with two children. He had encouraged neighborhood youngsters to consider him as a big brother who was available to counsel with them when they experienced problems. He felt comfortable with this role, whereas (as he later admitted) he had never felt relaxed with his peers; he felt himself to be, in a sense, "posing" as an adult.

The 13-year-old female, from a neglectful and abusive background, was overwhelmed by the attention and concern from an adult male. She developed a "crush" bordering on adoration.

He insisted, during our initial interview, that "It's not the way it might appear; she's really mature." He refused to consider as comparable the fact that he perceived his own 12-year-old daughter as still being a child. He would, he emphasized, never accept a man his age having a sexual relationship with her. The 13-year-old "victim," he insisted, was "different." He encouraged me to meet her, certain that I would see her as he did: a sophisticated, mature young adult. When I did meet her, I discovered a shy, chubby girl, looking closer to 11 or 12 than to 13. Sophistication was nowhere in evidence. Never underestimate the power of the phenomenon of age merging.

ANGER

Anger can be an obvious or subtle component in the matrix of precipitating factors (Mayer, 1988). Though it may not always be present, it is potent when activated. When physical violence is a part of the offense, it is likely that anger is present as a factor. However, the presence of physical violence signifies that the offender has inadequate control over his behavior and may present a significant risk of inappropriately acting out his anger; he would best be treated, if possible, in a residential setting.

The anger may be related to any of a number of issues, including loss of, or inability to find, employment; breakup of a relationship; extreme frustration at work; and/or dissatisfaction with a spouse. The offender seeks to reduce the anger-induced stress by sexual contact with a child. Treatment must help him first identify the actual focus of his anger and then learn to resolve (or accept) his frustration in an appropriate way.

In many cases, the anger is repressed. The offender presents in a rather passive, even submissive, manner. The therapist may as a result rather routinely eliminate the hypothesis that anger is an active component. Avoid this mistake. In your therapeutic probing, explore for areas of possible undue frustration in the offender's current (or developmental) experiences.

An offender had molested his stepdaughter, using gratuitous force and also directing hostile and derogatory verbal comments at her. It became clear during treatment that his behavior was largely based on his unresolved anger towards his wife's ex-husband (the victim's father). Exploring the relationship between this unresolved anger and the child molestation, it was revealed that the girl reminded him, both physically and symbolically, of the ex-husband (whom he knew and resented). During treatment, special emphasis was placed on helping him to understand and deal with his anger.

More frequently, even when anger is a relevant factor the offender's behavior is unlikely to evidence violence. Subtle (or, at times, blatant) manipulation of the victim is used. Such a behavioral style enables the offender to continue to deny his anger while perceiving himself in a positive manner. This may make it even more difficult to have him identify with his angry feelings, since he may readily note the care and concern he had shown for his victim's well-being. In such cases it will probably prove unwise to insist on demonstrating the connection between his anger and child molesting. Instead, deal with the anger as a seemingly separate issue. Use your own clinical judgment as to when the most appropriate time (least threatening for the offender) would be to pursue it therapeutically. The goal is to attempt to resolve all relevant issues, not to pursue primary treatment issues in an inflexible order.

STRESS

In most circumstances, we seek to reduce or eliminate, rather than endure, stress. If we are hungry, we eat. If we are lonely, we socialize. If we feel "closed-in" by urban life, we may visit the countryside. In these examples, as in any others that might be added, however, society indicates (whether explicitly or implicitly) appropriate ways in which to behave. If we are hungry, for example, we may not walk uninvited into someone else's home and "raid the refrigerator." We are expected to understand which behaviors, under which circumstances, are forbidden. Further, we are expected to possess or obtain the necessary skills to enable us to reduce our stress in an acceptable manner.

The offender may suffer from feelings of stress due to factors conceptually related to child molestation, such as need for affection or sexual frustration. Or he may be experiencing stress from factors such as job dissatisfaction, poor health, or poor finances. In either case, though, he seeks to reduce his stress in an inappropriate manner. In some cases (though certainly a minority), he may actually be ignorant of societal proscriptions (e.g., he may be from a more permissive subculture or a foreign culture). One of your tasks then may be to educate him as to societal rules, laws, and expectations.

Do not just assume that he understands what is expected of him. Despite his having been criminally prosecuted, there is no certainty that he clearly understands what was inappropriate about his behavior. He may, for example, believe that he was wrong for having fondled the victim under her clothing, concluding that it is permissible to fondle her over her clothing. His confusion may be further reinforced by the legal jargon used as his case moves through the criminal justice system. Terms such as "sexual assault," "child molestation," and "incest," for example, do not give a clear behavioral picture.

In other cases, he may be aware that his manner of stress reduction is inappropriate, even illegal, but not possess the necessary skills to satisfy his needs in an acceptable manner. In these cases, part of your job will be to help him develop such skills (usually, social skills) or at least to help him include such programming as part of his support system (Segal & Marshall, 1985; Whitman & Quinsey, 1981). In addition, it would be useful for him to learn stress-reduction techniques (Meichenbaum, 1985). Finally, he should be encouraged to talk with someone (such as a counselor) when he experiences significant stress in the future.

EMPATHY

Narcissism is a significant personality component of most

child molesters (Mayer, 1988). They are extremely sensitive to their own needs, desires, and discomfort. At the same time, they tend to be markedly insensitive to how their behavior affects others. They are readily able to blind themselves to the realities of their behavior and its effects on their victims ("The Sex Offender," 1988).

Not uncommonly, they may perceive their victim as an object. They are open to all sorts of rationalizations, such as convincing themselves that any lack of clear, direct protestation from the victim must indicate, at the least, consent. Difficult as it may be for most people to believe, some offenders are well able to convince themselves that even an infant (say, a 1-year-old) may have been sexually provocative, may have "teased" them.

This ability to misperceive his own behavior and its effects in such an extreme fashion tends to "protect" him from feeling adequately remorseful for his actions. The offender has portrayed himself in his own mind as benevolent, as someone who would never abuse a child. Thus, he is easily drawn to the conclusion that he did not in fact hurt anyone. The victim is seen as either a consentual partner or a fortunate recipient of affection and/or attention. In many cases, the offender may even focus on his perception that the "system" (i.e., social service, police, courts, etc.) is abusing the child. In any event, it would be folly to assume that, because he has been prosecuted, he must inevitably understand the trauma he may have created for the child. He may only believe he has "technically" broken the law. He will not be amenable to the development of empathetic concern for the victim as long as he is unaware of and does not understand issues of victimization (Annis, Mathers, & Baker, 1984). And until he feels a sense of empathy for victims and makes a connection between his behavior and the victimization process, he remains a higher risk for recidivism.

One practical and satisfactory way in which to have him gain some understanding of the effects of his behavior on his victim is to use audio-visual materials, such as published accounts by victims (Allen, 1980; Armstrong, 1978; Bass & Thornton, 1983), video recordings by victims, and dramatized presentations of victimization and its effects (see listing in Appendix, pp. 39-41).

If the diagnostic interview revealed that he himself had been sexually abused at one time, this should be explored and tied in with his own behavior. He needs to resolve whatever feelings (probably guilt, shame, and anger) may have been engendered by his own abuse and then understand the parallel trauma he has caused the victim (Lew, 1988; Porter, 1986). In any event, attempt to elicit from him descriptions (emphasize the affect involved) of his reactions to any victimization (sexual or otherwise) he has experienced during his life. Discuss them with him. Comment on and correct any rationalizations or minimizations he may use in relating the presented situations to his own.

VICTIM CONCERNS

As noted in the section on empathy (pp. 33-35), it is very important that the offender begin to develop some understanding of the effects abuse may have on the victim (Conte, 1985; Lindberg & Distad, 1985; Russell, 1984). First, assuming his offense was not clearly physically coercive, he will likely have difficulty in understanding why the victim did not object if she or he was not freely consenting. It is important in this regard that you be fully aware of the victim's statement. The victim may indeed have indicated unwillingness to engage in the abuse. Yet the offender may have misperceived the message. He may have had (and still may have) inappropriate, but often societally sanctioned, expectations that anything short of intense protest indicates consent. He needs to be more sensitive to the often subtle ways in which children are likely to signal their feelings when they are faced with conflict.

The offender must be made to understand that children are taught to submit to the will of adults; they are, in fact, often criticized and/or punished for challenging adult authority. Thus, the child may be unwilling or afraid to clearly convey her or his unwillingness to participate. In some cases, in fact, she or he may have become so sensitive to the wishes of adults that she or he will anticipate the adult's desire and "initiate" contact. Such behavior, unless clearly understood, is likely to validate the offender's inclination to believe his behavior is acceptable.

In some cases, when the child seems to be behaving in a sexually provocative manner, it may be a sign that she or he has already been a victim of sexual abuse (MacFarlane & Waterman, 1986). Rather than encouraging such behavior, the offender must learn that it is appropriate to discourage it (without being harsh or critical).

He needs to understand that his intrusive behavior may engender in the victim a sense of helplessness, a feeling of loss of control over her or his own body. This in turn may lead to experiencing a sense of depersonalization, possibly leading to long-term emotional dysfunction (Lusk & Waterman, 1986).

In discussing the above-noted issues, the offender may begin to experience feelings of guilt. This is positive and should not be discouraged or diffused. However, take care to see that it does not develop to a dysfunctional level. Overwhelming self-blame will likely discourage him from a willingness to reflect productively on his past thought-processes and behavior. The goal is to use the guilt as a motivational factor, to encourage introspection and self-monitoring, and to discourage future inappropriate fantasies and behavior.

LETTER OF APOLOGY

In many cases it will be seen as appropriate for the offender to write a letter of apology to the victim (Rencken, 1989). Though it may appear that such an action would be constructive for both the offender and the victim, there are some considerations of which you should be acutely aware.

First, keep in mind that the primary consideration must be for the welfare of the victim. Though it may be therapeutically beneficial for the offender to write such a letter, it may be that, for example, the abuse was so traumatic for the victim that she or he wishes to have absolutely no contact with the offender. If possible, it is always wise to consult with the victim's therapist or parent. It may also be necessary to get approval from the offender's probation agent because the rules of supervision may include a "no contact" provision.

Finally, assuming that all the preceding problems have been resolved, it is critical that the letter not be transmitted without your first having reviewed it and made any necessary changes.

In accord with the earlier comments regarding the narcissistic characteristics prevalent in child molesters, it is likely that the first draft of the letter of apology will focus on the needs of the offender. He is likely to write about all the grief he has suffered as a consequence of the abuse. After listing his troubles, he then may attempt to enlist the victim's sympathy and ask her or him to forgive him. This attempts to put the victim in the position of feeling guilty for all the hardship her or his abuse has caused the offender! Then, the victim is expected to disregard whatever feelings of anger she or he may still have and caretake the offender.

Review the letter with the offender, explaining to him any of the previous material which appears relevant. Help him rewrite the letter. The final version should be brief, with the offender acknowledging full responsibility for the abuse, reassuring the victim that she or he did nothing to provoke it. If the offense was discovered through the victim's report (rather than by some other means), the offender should note that he harbors no ill will for the victim having reported the abuse. Finally, it should state a clear apology without requesting forgiveness. If any forgiveness is to be given, it must be given freely by the victim, not upon request of the offender (which would have the effect of continued victimization).

RELAPSE PREVENTION

Increasingly, clinicians are recognizing that the offender is never "cured." There always remains some level of risk of recidivism, no matter how minimal it may be at any particular time. Thus, it is important that the offender learn to monitor his risk level (remember the "thermometer of risk") and take corrective action whenever appropriate (Laws, 1989; Pithers et al., 1983; Turkington, 1987).

There are essentially three formats under which this ongoing monitoring process may be implemented: individual meetings with a counselor, group meetings, and self-monitoring. Effectively, the offender must always be prepared to use the self-monitoring modality. Thus, the practical issue becomes one of deciding whether either (or both) of the remaining two modalities are necessary supplements and, if so, whether one is to be preferred.

Self-monitoring is necessary but not usually sufficient to satisfactorily minimize risk of recidivism (at least in the early period of relapse-prevention work). Meeting with an individual counselor may help in insuring that the client continues to self-monitor, but it is unlikely to introduce the variety of seemingly unrelated life experiences which may indirectly raise risk level. Group interaction has distinct advantages at this point.

At the relapse-prevention stage of treatment, the offender should already be aware of and understand the various factors which may contribute to risk enhancement. There is no longer any pressing need to focus meetings on these factors in a didactic fashion. Rather, it is important for the offender to participate in discussions of actual, ongoing life situations. He needs to learn and practice appropriate problem-solving techniques and reflect on how inappropriate ways of resolving such real-life difficulties increase the risk of recidivism. Group interaction offers this opportunity.

Because it is often difficult, if not impossible, to know at the outset whether any particular subject matter (brought up by a group member) may ultimately have any significant relevance to risk enhancement of child molestation, it is prudent for the facilitator to encourage a fairly wide latitude of subject matter as suitable for group discussion. Whatever problem areas are presented, insure that the group discussion leads to appropriate attempts at problem solving (rather than only sympathetic and/or empathetic reiteration of the problem). Then, facilitate some group closure on the particular problem by focusing on an understanding of how inappropriate resolution might tie in with one or more of the dynamic factors the group members learned in their primary treatment phase.

Ideally, such a support group should be available on an ongoing basis with each member having the option of showing up as needed (which may vary over time from regular to intermittent attendance). My experience suggests that a weekly meeting of 1-1/2 hours is satisfactory.

If a "sex offender" support group is unavailable (see listing of some groups in Appendix, pp. 39-41), it may be helpful for the offender to attend another support group (e.g., one for adult children of alcoholics), the critical issue being a forum in which to explore appropriate problem solving of day-to-day issues. In such a case, it may be helpful to occasionally supplement such meetings with individual counseling sessions focused on exploring and reinforcing the connection between whatever issues were discussed in group and the dynamics of child molestation.

Finally, it can be quite helpful, with permission of the offender, to have a meeting with a significant person in his life (such as a spouse). Provide this individual with a general understanding of what has gone on in treatment and encourage her or his helping the offender in his self-monitoring (Northwest Treatment Associates, undated). Assuming close daily contact, this person is in an ideal position to prompt the offender should he either not be aware of significant (and potentially troubling) situations or not engage in appropriate problem solving. A support group for such significant others is also helpful (see listing in Appendix, pp. 39-41).

APPENDIX

VIDEOS ABOUT VICTIMS

Breaking Silence - Film Distribution Center, 1028 Industry Drive, Seattle, WA 98188.

An award-winning film on incest and the sexual abuse of children.

Incest: The Victim Nobody Believes - AIMS Media, 6901 Woodley Avenue, Van Nuys, CA 91406.

Candid discussions with three young women who convey what it is really like to be caught in a web of fear, confusion, and guilt.

The Last Taboo - AIMS Media, 6901 Woodley Avenue, Van Nuys, CA 91406.

Testimonials from six childhood sexual abuse victims.

Men Who Molest/Children Who Survive - Filmmakers Library, Inc., 133 E. 58 Street, New York, NY 10022.

Filmed at Northwest Treatment Associates in Seattle, Washington, this gives an intimate look at four child molesters who tell what they did and why they did it. Includes observation of their treatment, and child survivors speaking for themselves.

To a Safer Place - AIMS Media, 6901 Woodley Avenue, Van Nuys, CA 91406.

Video about the sexual abuse by her father of a girl from infancy to early adolescence.

Why, God - Why Me? - Varied Directions, 69 Elm Street, Camden, ME 04843.

Video which dramatizes the true life story of a single woman who triumphed over the trauma of childhood sexual abuse.

AUDIOCASSETTE ABOUT CHILD SEXUAL ABUSE

Crime of Silence: The Sexual Abuse of Children - Janice Ball or Portia Franklin, P.O. Box B, Old Chelsea Station, New York, NY 10011.

A radio documentary from National Public Radio. It features accounts from victims and offenders, as well as health care specialists, legal professionals, social workers, and psychologists. Participants describe the scope of the problem, some of the devastating effects on victims, and promising strategies for treatment and prevention.

SOURCES FOR MATERIALS DEALING WITH CHILD MOLESTATION

National Committee for Prevention of Child Abuse - Attention: Publishing Department, P.O. Box 94283, Chicago, IL 60690.

Distributors of *You Don't Have To Molest That Child* (Timothy Smith, 1987). This booklet is designated specifically for child molesters, challenging them to admit they have a serious problem and urging them to seek help. "A suggested plan to help people recognize and correct their behavior is included as part of the strategy to stop sexual abuse at its source."

Project for the Advancement of Sexual Health and Safety, Inc. - P.O. Box 272, Thomaston, ME 04861.

Distributors of *Child Sexual Abuse, Protecting Kids by Knowing the Abusers* (1985). Written by incarcerated felons who are participants in the Maine State Prison Sex Offender Project. All the writers have a history of sexual assaultiveness towards children and/or adults. The booklet is intended for adults. Some of the topics covered are the vulnerability of children; manipulation of the environment by the molester; how molesters get the child not to tell.

SUPPORT ORGANIZATIONS

CO-S.A. - P.O. Box 14537, Minneapolis, MN 55414. Telephone - (612) 537-6904.

A 12-step based program for people who are or have been in a relationship with a sex addict (not necessarily an abuser).

Institute for the Community As Extended Family - P.O. Box 952, San Jose, CA 95108. Telephone - (408) 280-5055.

Provides information about the Child Sexual Abuse Treatment Program of Santa Clara, California. Started in 1971 by H. Giarretto, PhD, this program was one of the first in the country. The institute also can provide information about several nationally organized self-help groups: Adults Molested as Children; Parents United; and Daughters and Sons United.

National Association on Sexual Addiction Problems - 22937 Arlington Avenue, Suite 201, Torrance, CA 90501.

S-ANON - P.O. Box 5517, Sherman Oaks, CA 91413. Telephone - (818) 990-6910.

Sex Addicts Anonymous - P.O. Box 3038, Minneapolis, MN 55403. Telephone - (612) 871-1520.

Sex and Love Addicts Anonymous - P.O. Box 529, Newton, MA 02258. Telephone - (617) 332-1845.

Sexaholics Anonymous - P.O. Box 300, Simi Valley, CA 93062. Telephone - (805) 581-3343.

PROFESSIONAL ORGANIZATIONS

American Professional Society on the Abuse of Children - University of Chicago, School of Social Service Administration, 969 East 60th, Chicago, IL 60637.

Association for the Behavioral Treatment of Sexual Abusers - P.O. Box 66028, Portland, OR 97266.

REFERENCES

Abrams, S. (1989). Probation polygraph surveillance of child abusers. *The Prosecutor (Journal of the National District Attorneys Association), 22,* 29-38.

Allen, C. (1980). *Daddy's Girl.* New York: Berkley.

American Psychiatric Association. (1987). *Diagnostic and Statistical Manual of Mental Disorders* (3rd ed. rev.). Washington, DC: Author.

American Psychological Association. (1981). Ethical principles of psychologists. *American Psychologist, 36,* 633-638.

Annis, L., Mathers, L., & Baker, C. (1984). Victim workers as therapists for incarcerated sex offenders. *Victimology: An International Journal, 9,* 426-435.

Annon, J., & Robinson, C. (1989). *Assessment and Treatment of Sex Offenders: A Videotape Training Program.* Grand Island, NE: Farrall Instruments, Inc.

Armstrong, L. (1978). *Kiss Daddy Goodnight.* New York: Hawthorn.

Barnard, G., Fuller, A. K., Robbins, L., & Shaw, T. (1989). *The Child Molester: An Integrated Approach to Evaluation and Treatment.* New York: Brunner/Mazel.

Bass, E., & Thornton, L. (1983). *I Never Told Anyone: Writings by Women Survivors of Child Sexual Abuse.* New York: Harper & Row.

Bays, L., & Freeman-Longo, R. (1989). *Why Did I Do It Again? Understanding My Cycle of Problem Behaviors.* Orwell, VT: Safer Society.

Becker, J., Kaplan, M., Cunningham-Rathner, J., & Kavoussi, R. (1986). Characteristics of adolescent incest sexual perpetrators: Preliminary findings. *Journal of Family Violence, 1,* 85-97.

Brodsky, S. (1977). The mental health professional on the witness stand: A survival guide. In B. D. Sales (Ed.), *Psychology in the Legal Process* (pp. 269-276). New York: Spectrum.

Carnes, P. (1983). *Out of the Shadows.* Minneapolis: CompCare.

Carnes, P. (1989). *Contrary to Love: Helping the Sexual Addict.* Minneapolis: CompCare.

CompCare. (1987). *Hope & Recovery: A Twelve Step Guide for Healing from Compulsive Sexual Behavior.* Minneapolis: Author.

Conte, J. (1985). The effects of sexual abuse on children: A critique and suggestions for future research. *Victimology: An International Journal, 10,* 110-130.

Cook, M., & Howells, K. (Eds.). (1981). *Adult Sexual Interest in Children.* New York: Academic Press.

Emmerman, L. (1985, May 29). A self-confessed pedophile: 'I wish it would all end.' *Chicago Tribune*, pp. 1, 3.

Finkelhor, D. (1984). *Child Sexual Abuse: New Theory & Research.* New York: Free Press.

Finkelhor, D. (1986). *A Sourcebook on Child Sexual Abuse.* Newbury Park, CA: Sage.

Finkelhor, D., & Araji, S. (1986). Explanations of pedophilia: A four factor model. *Journal of Sex Research, 22,* 145-161.

Finkelhor, D., & Browne, A. (1985). The traumatic impact of child sexual abuse: A conceptualization. *American Journal of Orthopsychiatry, 55,* 530-541.

Freeman-Longo, R., & Bays, L. (1988). *Who Am I and Why Am I in Treatment? A Guided Workbook for Clients in Evaluation and Beginning Treatment.* Orwell, VT: Safer Society.

Friedman, S. (1989). Criminal investigation and clinical assessment in child sexual abuse cases: Making a distinction. *The Advisor, 2,* 16-17.

Friedrich, W. (in press). Child abuse and sex abuse. In R. L. Greene (Ed.), *The M.M.P.I.: Use in Specific Diagnostic Groups.* New York: Grune & Stratton.

Gable, R. (1986). Prediction of dangerousness and implications for treatment. In W. Curran, A. McGarry, & S. Shah (Eds.), *Forensic Psychiatry and Psychology* (pp. 129-144). Philadelphia: F. A. Davis.

Greer, J., & Stuart, I. (Eds.). (1983). *The Sexual Aggressor: Current Perspectives on Treatment.* New York: Van Nostrand Reinhold.

Grisso, T., & Seigel, S. (1986). Assessment of competency to stand criminal trial. In W. Curran, A. McGarry, & S. Shah (Eds.), *Forensic Psychiatry and Psychology* (pp. 145-165). Philadelphia: F. A. Davis.

Hall, G., Maiuro, R., Vitaliano, P., & Proctor, W. (1986). The utility of the MMPI with men who have sexually assaulted children. *Journal of Consulting and Clinical Psychology, 54,* 494-496.

Hobson, W., & Bunk, B. (1987). Assessment and treatment of men who commit sexual offenses. In P. A. Keller & S. R. Heyman (Eds.), *Innovations in Clinical Practice: A Source Book* (Vol. 6, pp. 121-129). Sarasota, FL: Professional Resource Exchange.

Hucker, S., Langevin, R., Wortzman, G., Bain, J., Handy, J., Chambers, J., & Wright, S. (1986). Neurological impairment in pedophiles. *Canadian Journal of Behavioral Science, 18,* 440-448.

Hucker, S. J., Webster, C. D., & Ben-Aron, M. H. (Eds.). (1981). *Mental Disorder and Criminal Responsibility.* Toronto: Butterworth.

Jacobs, J. (undated). *Drinking and Crime* (NCJ 97221). Washington, DC: National Institute of Justice.

Jagim, R., Wittman, W., & Noll, J. (1978). Mental health professionals' attitudes toward confidentiality, privilege, and third party disclosure. *Professional Psychology, 9,* 458-466.

Kaplan, G. (1988). *Inpatient vs. Outpatient vs. Non-Amenable to Treatment.* (Available from Alpha Human Services, 2712 Fremont Avenue S., Minneapolis, MN 55408.)

Knight, R. A., Carter, D. L., & Prentky, R. A. (1989). A system for the classification of child molesters: Reliability and application. *Journal of Interpersonal Violence, 4,* 3-23.

Knopp, F. H. (1984). *Retraining Adult Sex Offenders: Methods and Models* . Orwell, VT: Safer Society.

Knopp, F. H., Rosenberg, J., & Stevenson, W. (1986). *Report on Nationwide Survey of Juvenile & Adult Sex-Offender Treatment Programs and Providers.* Orwell, VT: Safer Society.

Kourany, R. C., Hill, R. Y., & Hollender, M. H. (1986). The age of sexual consent. *Bulletin of the American Academy of Psychiatry and Law, 14,* 171-176.

Lanning, K. (1986). *Child Molesters: A Behavioral Analysis for Law-Enforcement Officers Investigating Cases of Child Sexual Exploitation* (2-86-005). Washington, DC: National Center for Missing and Exploited Children.

Lanyon, R. (1986a). Psychological assessment procedures in court-related settings. *Professional Psychology: Research and Practice, 17,* 260-268.

Lanyon, R. (1986b). Theory and treatment in child molestation. *Journal of Consulting and Clinical Psychology, 54,* 176-182.

Laws, D. R. (1985). Sexual fantasy alternation: Procedural considerations. *Journal of Behavior Therapy & Experimental Psychiatry, 16,* 39-44.

Laws, D. R. (1988). Treating pedophiles in the community. *Preventing Sexual Abuse, 1,* 8-11.

Laws, D. R. (Ed.). (1989). *Relapse Prevention with Sex Offenders*. New York: Guilford.

Levin, S. M., & Stava, L. (1987). Personality characteristics of sex offenders: A review. *Archives of Sexual Behavior, 16,* 57-79.

Lew, M. (1988). *Victims No Longer: Men Recovering from Incest and Other Sexual Child Abuse*. New York: Nevraumont.

Lindberg, F. H., & Distad, L. J. (1985). Post-traumatic stress disorders in women who experienced childhood incest. *Child Abuse & Neglect, 9,* 329-334.

Lusk, R., & Waterman, J. (1986). Effects of sexual abuse on children. In K. MacFarlane & J. Waterman (Eds.), *Sexual Abuse of Young Children* (pp. 101-118). New York: Guilford.

MacFarlane, K., & Waterman, J. (1986). *Sexual Abuse of Young Children*. New York: Guilford.

Mayer, A. (1988). *Sex Offenders: Approaches to Understanding and Management*. Holmes Beach, FL: Learning Publications.

McGuire, J. M., Toal, P., & Blau, B. (1985). The adult client's conception of confidentiality in the therapeutic relationship. *Professional Psychology: Research and Practice, 16,* 375-384.

Meichenbaum, D. (1985). *Stress Inoculation Training*. New York: Pergamon.

Melton, G. B., & Limber, S. (1989). Psychologists' involvement in cases of child maltreatment. *American Psychologist, 44,* 1225-1233.

Money, J. (1986). *Lovemaps*. New York: Irvington.

Money, J. (1987). Treatment guidelines: Antiandrogen and counseling of paraphilic sex offenders. *Journal of Sex & Marital Therapy, 13,* 219-223.

Moore, H. A., Zusman, J., & Root, G. C. (1985). Noninstitutional treatment for sex offenders in Florida. *American Journal of Psychiatry, 142,* 964-967.

Muehleman, T., & Kimmons, C. (1981). Psychologists' views on child abuse reporting, confidentiality, life and the law: An exploratory study. *Professional Psychology, 12,* 631-638.

Newlund, S. (1985). Sex offenders defend jail as punishment. *St. Paul Pioneer Press,* pp. 1, 12.

Nichols, H. R., & Molinder, I. (1984). *Multiphasic Sex Inventory Manual.* (Available from Nichols and Molinder, 437 Bowes Drive, Tacoma, WA 98466.)

Northwest Treatment Associates. (undated). *Partner Alert Lists.* Seattle, WA: Author.

O'Brien, S. (1986). *Why They Did It: Stories of Eight Convicted Child Molesters.* Springfield, IL: Charles C. Thomas.

O'Connell, M. (1986). Reuniting incest offenders with their families. *Journal of Interpersonal Violence, 1,* 374-386.

Paveza, G. (1988). Risk factors in father-daughter child sexual abuse: A case-controlled study. *Journal of Interpersonal Violence, 3,* 290-306.

Peters Institute. (undated). *A Ten-Year Follow-Up of Sex Offender Recidivism.* Philadelphia: Author. (Joseph J. Peters Institute, 260 S. Broad St., Ste. 220, Philadelphia, PA 19102.)

Pithers, W., & Gibat, C. (1985). *Annotated Bibliography Regarding Penile Plethysmography.* (Available from Department of Corrections, Chittenden Community Correctional Center, 7 Farrell Street, South Burlington, VT 05401.)

Pithers, W., Marques, J., Gibat, C., & Marlatt, G. (1983). Relapse prevention with sexual aggressives: A self-control model of treatment and maintenance of change. In J. Greer & I. Stuart (Eds.), *The Sexual Aggressor: Current Perspectives on Treatment* (pp. 214-230). New York: Van Nostrand Reinhold.

Porter, E. (1986). *Treating the Young Male Victim of Sexual Assault.* Orwell, VT: Safer Society.

Quinsey, V. (1983). Prediction of recidivism and the evaluation of treatment programs for sex offenders. In S. N. Verdun-Jones & A. A. Keltner (Eds.), *Sexual Aggression and the Law* (pp. 28-40). Simon Fraser University: Criminology Research Centre.

Quinsey, V. (1986). Men who have sex with children. In D. N. Weisstub (Ed.), *Law and Mental Health: International Perspectives* (pp. 140-172). New York: Pergamon.

Quinsey, V., Arnold, L., & Pruesse, M. (1980). MMPI profiles of men referred for a pretrial psychiatric assessment as a function of offense type. *Journal of Clinical Psychology, 36,* 410-417.

Rencken, R. H. (1989). *Intervention Strategies for Sexual Abuse.* Alexandria, VA: American Association for Counseling and Development.

Rouleau, J., Kaplan, M., & Reich, J. (1984). *The Treatment of Child Molesters.* (Available from Columbia University, SBC-TM, 722 W. 168 Street, Box 17, New York, NY 10032.)

Rowan, E. L., & Rowan, J. B. (1985). Developing a treatment program for pedophiles. *Corrective and Social Psychiatry, 31,* 62-64.

Russell, D. E. H. (1984). *Sexual Exploitation: Rape, Child Sexual Abuse, and Workplace Harassment.* Newbury Park, CA: Sage.

Salter, A. C. (1988). *Treating Child Sex Offenders and Victims: A Practical Guide.* Newbury Park, CA: Sage.

Segal, Z. V., & Marshall, W. L. (1985). Heterosexual social skills in a population of rapists and child molesters. *Journal of Consulting and Clinical Psychology, 53,* 55-63.

The sex offender as criminal thinker. (1988). *Preventing Sexual Abuse, 1,* 4-7, 12.

Shelton, J. L., & Levy, R. L. (1981). *Behavioral Assignments and Treatment Compliance: A Handbook of Clinical Strategies.* Champaign, IL: Research Press.

Smith, T. A. (1985). Developing your theoretical framework. *Sexual Violence Quarterly, 1,* 4-5.

Smith, T. A., & Conte, J. R. (1986). What can offenders teach us about prevention? *Preventing Sexual Abuse, 1,* 1-3.

Smith, W. R., & Monastersky, C. (1986). Assessing juvenile sexual offenders' risk for reoffending. *Criminal Justice and Behavior, 13,* 115-140.

Thorne, F. C. (1986). *The Sex Inventory.* (Available from Clinical Psychology Publishing Company, Inc., 4 Conant Square, Brandon, VT 05733.)

Trepper, T. S., & Barrett, M. J. (Eds.). (1986). *Treating Incest: A Multimodal Systems Perspective.* New York: Haworth Press.

Turkington, C. (1987, March). Sexual aggression 'widespread.' *APA Monitor*, pp. 15-17.

Wakefield, H., & Underwager, R. (1988). *Accusations of Child Sexual Abuse.* Springfield, IL: Charles C. Thomas.

Wegner, D. (1989). *White Bears and Other Unwanted Thoughts: Suppression, Obsession, and the Psychology of Mental Control.* New York: Viking.

Whitman, W. P., & Quinsey, V. L. (1981). Heterosocial skill training for institutionalized rapists and child molesters. *Canadian Journal of Behavioral Science, 13,* 105-114.

Wolf, S. C. (1984, November). *A Multi-Factor Model of Deviant Sexuality.* Paper presented at the Third International Conference on Victimology, Lisbon, Portugal. (Available from Northwest Treatment Associates, 315 West Galer Street, Seattle, WA 98119.)

Wolf, S. C. (Ed.). (1985). *Sexual Violence Quarterly, 1.* (Available from Sexual Violence Quarterly, 315 West Galer Street, Seattle, WA 98119.)

Yalom, I. D. (1975). *The Theory and Practice of Group Psychotherapy* (2nd ed.). New York: Basic Books.

OTHER TITLES IN THE PRACTITIONER'S RESOURCE SERIES

Outpatient Treatment of Child Molesters is one of nine books now available in the Practitioner's Resource Series. The other published titles are:

Clinical Guidelines for Involuntary Outpatient Treatment by J. Reid Meloy, Ansar Haroun, and Eugene F. Schiller.
(IOTH) Paperback: $9.95 1990 78pp.
ISBN #0-943158-45-1

Cognitive Therapy for Personality Disorders: A Schema-Focused Approach by Jeffrey E. Young.
(CTPDH) Paperback: $9.95 1990 90pp.
ISBN #0-943158-46-X

Dealing with Anger Problems: Rational-Emotive Therapeutic Interventions by Windy Dryden.
(DAPH) Paperback: $9.95 1990 62pp.
ISBN #0-943158-59-1

Diagnosis and Treatment Selection for Anxiety Disorders by Samuel Knapp and Leon VandeCreek.
(DTSH) Paperback: $9.95 1989 94pp.
ISBN #0-943158-30-3

Neuropsychological Evaluation of Head Injury by Lawrence C. Hartlage.
(NEHIH) Paperback: $9.95 1990 68pp.
ISBN #0-943158-47-8

Pre-Employment Screening for Psychopathology: A Guide to Professional Practice by Rodney L. Lowman.
(PESH) Paperback: $9.95 1989 86pp.
ISBN #0-943158-34-6

Tarasoff and Beyond: Legal and Clinical Considerations in the Treatment of Life-Endangering Patients by Leon VandeCreek and Samuel Knapp.

(TABH) Paperback: $9.95 1989 74pp.
ISBN #0-943158-31-1

What Every Therapist Should Know About AIDS by Samuel Knapp and Leon VandeCreek.

(AIDSH) Paperback: $9.95 1990 80pp.
ISBN #0-943158-58-3

The following book will be available soon:

Assessment and Treatment of Multiple Personality and Dissociative Disorders by James P. Bloch.

(ATMH) Paperback: $9.95 Avail. Spring 1991 Approx. 92 pp.
ISBN #0-943158-67-2

SHIPPING CHARGES
Up to $15.99 Order, Add $1.75 in US, $3.00 Foreign
$16-$30.99 Order, Add $2.75 in US, $4.00 Foreign
$31-$45.99 Order, Add $3.75 in US, $5.00 Foreign
$46-$70.99 Order, Add $4.25 in US, $6.00 Foreign
Orders over $70, Add 7% in US, 10% Foreign
For 1- & 2-Day Air Service, Call for Charges

If you would like to order or receive more information on any of these publications, please call **813-366-7913** or write Professional Resource Exchange, Inc., P.O. Box 15560-H, Sarasota, FL 34277-1560, and we will be happy to send you our latest newsletter/catalog. When you call or write, please tell us your professional affiliation (e.g., Psychologist, Clinical Social Worker, Marriage and Family Therapist, Mental Health Counselor, School Psychologist, Psychiatrist, etc.) to be assured of receiving all appropriate mailings.

We are dedicated to providing you with applied resources and up-to-date information that you can immediately use in your practice. Our orders are usually shipped within 2 working days and come with a 15 day no-questions-asked money back guarantee. (Availability and prices subject to change without notice.)

Thanks for your interest!

Sincerely,

Lawrence G. Ritt, PhD
President